This is Just to Say
Meditations on a Theme by William Carlos Williams

David Breeden

D1714522

VIRTUAL ARTISTS COLLECTIVE
http://vacpoetry.org
ISBN: 978-0-9819898-0-8

This series of poems is dedicated to my son Patrick, who inspired the idea.

Part One: Transgression

A Note from YHWH...9
I Have Eaten...10
The Plums 11
That Were In 12
The Icebox...13
A Note from the Serpent..14

Part Two: Empathy or Epiphany

Another Note from the Serpent.......................................17
And Which...18
I have eaten the plums that were in the Icebox..................19
You Were Probably..20
Saving..21
For Breakfast 22
Another Word with the Serpent......................................23

Part Three: Prayer and Absolution

A Note from Eve to Adam..27
Prayer..28
Forgive Me...29
and which you were probably saving for breakfast 30
They Were Delicious 31
So Sweet 32
And So Cold...33
A Note from YHWH to the other Gods............................34
A Note to YHWH from Eve 35
Another Note from the Serpent......................................36
A Note to YHWH from the Other Gods............................37
A Note from Snakes...39

Part Four: The Fruit of the Knowledge

Forgive me they were delicious so sweet and so cold........43
This Is Just to Say 43
This is to Say...45
This is Just to Say...46

Part Five: Conclusion, a performance poem

I. Transgression.. 49
II. Empathy or Epiphany 50
III. Prayer and absolution 52

Part One: Transgression

A Note from YHWH

This is just to say
It is strictly
Explicitly
Forbidden
Off limits

That tree
That is in
The middle
The center of
The garden

The tree with fruit
Looking so luscious
So good to eat

That tree
It is forbidden
Off limits

Do not
Do not eat

Thereof

Punishable
Punishable by death
Which you do not know
And you don't want to

I Have Eaten

In the wilderness of words
Baudelaire's hideout
Mallarme's lair
It is the symbolic order
That is the forest for the trees

It is the language, unrealized
Waiting for a book
Indicating nothing

In the trees of the word
Mallarme's bee buzzes
A basket of symbol
A picnic of signified
And only a dream of lace

In the forest of the word
Somewhere is Baudelaire's dream
Bad flowers, frightened wine
The Palace of the Real
With pillars named

All named, each referring
Only to itself
Where meaning stops

The Plums

Let's call it guilt then
This human ailment

I'm not enough
I've done too much
I did, I did exactly
What I wished not to

Let's call it trying then
When we miss the mark
And let's call it what it is
– irritating like a fly buzz

Hurtful, crushed fruit
Hard rain on salt

What might have changed
Yet fruit, fruit is the center

That Were In

What was
The point
It was you were
Making?

You really
Made your
Point whatever
It was you were
Making

Your point
So important
Such clarity
To make

What was
The point
It was you were
Making?

The Icebox

Just a jokester
A trickster
A Faustus

Sold his soul
At the usual
Crossroads

In the usual way
– Mischief with fruits
Vegetables, desire

Looking where
He needed not to

The common tragedy
Adding up
To the usual uncommon

Story
Not him
More like us

A Note from the Serpent

This is just to say
YHWH is always

Making rules
That make as much

Sense as giraffes
That saunter

Around and
Who wants

Arbitrary rules
When YES sounds

So much better
On the lips

Part Two: Empathy or Epiphany

Another Note from the Serpent

This is just to say
But seriously folks

Knowledge of good
And evil? What's

To fear in that?
Do you people

Want to be
Like the other

Animals caught
Forever in impulse

Or do you want
A chance to consider?

And Which

I touch these pages
Damp in winter

I pace then—
As if awaiting hanging
As if awaiting death

As if
Only so much
As another day

I have eaten the plums that were in the Icebox

In the wilderness of words
Mallarme's hideout
Baudelaire's lair
It is the symbolic order
That is the forest for the trees

It is the language, unrealized
Waiting for a book
Indicating nothing

In the trees of the word
Mallarme's bee buzzes
A basket of symbol
A picnic of signified
And only a dream of lace

In the forest of the word
Somewhere is Baudelaire's dream
Bad flowers, frightened wine
The Palace of the Real
With pillars named

All named, each referring
Only to itself
Where meaning stops

You Were Probably

It is order that is upset
Order we didn't know

How pious are plums?
As plumb as. . .?

Order is how bodies fall
From the heads of

Pencils, from brush
Strokes and words

Saving

What is the music
What are the notes

Left out

Cut off
Ignored

At each note
Chosen?

For Breakfast

In a dream just over
I know now that

I climbed to the dome of this sky
And I swirled these clouds
In this life

And I have known
And waited for you

I have lived this life
For you though
I didn't know

Not until this dream
Was over

Now, now I know
In this moment
I climbed this dome of sky
For you in this life

And I reach
Now to swirl
The clouds for you

Another Word with the Serpent

This is just to say
This tree looks
Good for food
Pleasant to the eyes

A tree to be desired
Fruit to make one wise

Grasp the fruit
Go ahead, eat

Your eyes shall be
Opened and you
Shall be as gods
Knowing good

Knowing evil

Part Three: Prayer and Absolution

A Note from Eve to Adam

This is just to say
I have eaten
The fruit
That was in
The middle

Of the garden
And which
You were probably
Afraid
To taste

Forgive me
It was delicious
So sweet
And so cold

Prayer

Dear spouse who is out somewhere
You know I honor and cherish you

When you return
Chaos will retreat
From this kitchen
From this home

You gave me this day
Some delicious plums
Forgive my trespassing

You know I would forgive yours

I was led into temptation
Temptation I could not bear

You were saving them for breakfast
I knew you were saving them for breakfast

Forgive me

Forgive Me

What will be the dust
(Is it ours? Is it us?)
That at the last

We sweep
Below the rug?
If angels cry

At done and undone
What does that
Mean for tears?

Are they endless
Then? Or only
Like us?

and which you were probably saving for breakfast

In the wilderness of words
Baudelaire's hideout
In the forest of the word

Somewhere is Baudelaire's dream
Bad flowers, frightened wine
Dogs and lovers rotting
Along every road traveled

The Palace of the Real

With pillars named
All named, each referring
Only to itself
Where meaning stops

And each meant
Each thing meant
To be in a book

They Were Delicious

And there I was
Not going with the flow
Not trusting
Edges to soften

I make my aged hands go
Out to coffee cup
Out to plums
Open to mediate

How can it be?
I ask myself
Old man, that you
Don't know yet

The cup
The coffee
The coffee gone
From the cup

The plums
The stems

Where is it, old man
You forget and forget
The joy of going
With the damned flow

So Sweet

It may go without saying
That I'm hollow and hungry

It might be understood that
The dive I took
Keeps me swimming

It could be you know that
The void I embraced

Hugged me back

And So Cold

In the wilderness of words
Eliot's hideout
Williams' lair
It is the symbolic order
That is the forest for the trees

It is the language, unrealized
Waiting for a book
Indicating nothing

In the trees of the word
Eliot's ship wanders
A privateer of symbol
A pirate of signified
And only a dream of peace

In the forest of the word
Somewhere is Williams' dream
Luscious plums, delighted tasting
The Icebox of the Real
With restitution named

All named, each referring
Only to joy
Where meaning stops

33

A Note from YHWH to the other Gods

This is just to say
I was walking
In the garden
And the humans

Were hiding
Hiding among trees
Having eaten the fruit
That we. . .I forbade
Knowing too much

This is just to say
This is unforgivable
This knowing
So sweet
And so cold

A Note to YHWH from Eve

This is just to say
I have eaten the fruit
That you had mentioned

Something about
Death
And not eating thereof

Forgive me
Now I know
It was none
Of your business

Another Note from the Serpent

This Is Just to Say
Arbitrary law
May become
Justice

Plums
Hopes
For breakfast
The gifts

Of knowledge
Forgive us
Forgive us
Mostly because
We need no

Forgiveness

A Note to YHWH from the Other Gods

Everything (as you well know)
Is nowhere and nowhere
Everywhere (as you know)
The all-pervading perfection
You know beyond it all

As you well know
There is nothing more
Than nothing which
Is everything and more
Than everything and perhaps
Not even perfection at all
As you well know

These are after all
The simplicities of perfection
As you know

Your wishes
Your name
Our names
Our wishes
Pass through forests
And sounds that
Are never ours

And our selves
Constricted in
Symbol

The sounds of sounds
That are never things
As you know well
Know well

The simple-ness of complexity
Complexity in line
On line of words
Linear and a circle
You know as well spoken
In love as law

A Note from Snakes

This is just to say
A snake lime green
Cracking in age

Curls around a branch
To take on
Another skin

We snakes
Better than most
Know renewal

Then there is Eve
Grabbing fruit
In the eternal is

Before there was
A then

39

Part Four: The Fruit of the Knowledge

Forgive me they were delicious so sweet and so cold

In the wilderness of words
Mallarme's hideout

It is the language, unrealized
Waiting for a book
Indicating nothing

In the trees of the word
Mallarme's bee buzzes
A basket of symbol
A picnic of signified
And only a dream of lace

In the water of the word
Mallarme's swan beats
The chilling possible
Flight, mistakes, oblivion

All named, each referring
Only to itself
Where meaning freezes
Where meaning stops

43

This Is Just to Say

I have eaten
the fruit
that was on
the tree

and which
you for some reason
said
was forbidden

Forgive me
is was delicious
so sweet
and so cold

This is to Say

Absolution is impossible
Both ends being wrong

The forgiver to forgive
The transgressor transgressing

It is only our selves
We betray
We sin against
Our essences
Our natures

The gardens
The serpents
The gods

Stop gaps
Symbols
Words and words

For exploring
Our selves
Ourselves

45

This is Just to Say

In the wilderness of words
Baudelaire, Mallarme
Eliot, Williams

It is the symbolic order
That is the forest for the trees

In the trees of the word
Mallarme's bee buzzes
Baudelaire's bad flowers bloom

In the trees of the word
Eliot's ship wanders
In the forest of the word
Somewhere is Williams' dream

Luscious plums
Delighted tasting
The Icebox of the Real

All named, each referring
Only to joy
Where meaning stops

Where meaning stops

Part Five: Conclusion, a performance poem

NOTE: items in bold to be in unison with at least two other readers

I. Transgression

**I have eaten
the plums
that were in
the icebox**

I took the plums
I tasted the fruit
I yielded to the tug
Of transgression

I ate the plums
I turned them from
"Are" to "were"
Don't look for them here
They are no longer
In the icebox

They have joined
Poor, fallen human flesh
They are mine
And can be no one else's
Transgression occurred

II. Empathy or Epiphany

**and which
you were probably
saving
for breakfast**

The plums have been
Eaten—

        No—I ate
The plums

I acted

Consciously
Cog-ni-zant-ly
Knowing
        full well
Now was not the
Intention

Knowing full well
I was not the person

Knowing full well
You forbade the plums

Knowing full well
"Probably" has
Nothing to do
With the case

Probably, probably. . .
No—knowing full well

But more
That it was you
Your intention
Your saving
That I transgressed

III. Prayer and absolution

Forgive me
they were delicious
so sweet
and so cold

So delicious
(Forgive me)
So sweet
(they were delicious)
So cold
(so sweet)
Forgive me
(and so cold)

The icebox inviting
And breakfast may
Or may not come

So delicious
(Forgive me)
Now
(they <u>were</u> delicious)
This moment

So sweet
(so sweet)
I have eaten the plums
(and so cold)

So cold

52

(Forgive me)
They were fruit transfigured
(they were delicious)

All for me
(Forgive me)
All now
(they were delicious)

I am human
(Forgive me)

So delicious
(Forgive me)
So sweet
(they were delicious)
So cold
(so sweet)
Forgive me
(and so cold)

Forgive me
This Is Just to Say
Forgive me
I have eaten
the plums
Forgive me

that were in
the icebox

and which
you were probably
saving
for breakfast

Forgive me
they were delicious
so sweet
and so cold

David Breeden has an MFA from The Writers' Workshop at the University of Iowa, a Ph.D. from the Center for Writers at the University of Southern Mississippi, with additional study at Breadloaf and in writing and Buddhism at Naropa Institute in Boulder, Colorado. He also has a Master of Divinity from Meadville Lombard Theological School in Chicago.

His poetry, essays, and short fiction have appeared in such journals as *Mississippi Review, Nebo, Poet Lore, Mid-American Review,, North Atlantic Review, Boston Literary Review, Turnstile, Nidus,* and *Paragraph.* He has published four novels and nine books of poetry.

Breeden is a parish minister in Wisconsin.

Printed in the United States
215399BV00001B/31/P

9 780981 989808